Burning the Empty Nests

Poems by
Gregory Orr

Burning the Empty Nests

Harper & Row, Publishers
New York, Evanston, San Francisco, London

Grateful acknowledgment is made to the following magazines in which some of these poems first appeared: *Antaeus, Antioch Review, Arion's Dolphin, Ark River Review, Columbia Review, Epoch, First Issue, Hawaii Literary Review, The Lamp in the Spine, Lillabulero, The Little Review, New York Quarterly, The Seventies, TransPacific,* and *Trellis.*

"The Doll" first appeared in *Intro #3,* edited with an introduction by R. V. Cassill. Copyright © 1970 by Bantam Books, Inc. Reprinted by permission.

FIRST EDITION

Designed by Gloria Adelson

Library of Congress Cataloging in Publication Data

Orr, Gregory.
   Burning the empty nests.
I. Title.
PS3565.R7B8   811'.5'4   72-9143
ISBN 0-06-013241-8
ISBN 0-06-013243-4 (pbk.)

For Trisha
and for my Father
and Bernadette

Contents

4 The Adventures of the Stone

1

When We Are Lost

Darkness surrounds the dead tree. Gathering around it,
we set a torch to the trunk.
High in the branches sits an old man
made of wax. He wears a garland of wounds;
each one glows like a white leaf with its own light.
Flames rise toward him, and as they touch his feet
he explodes, scattering insects made of black glass.
A moth lands on the toe of my boot.
Picking it up, I discover a map on its wings.

3

Now

for Andrew Hoffman

Birds settle on my shoulders like dark epaulets.
The plants lift the green shields of their leaves,
and we march all night through the forest.
As we approach the town, its clocks
drift toward us. Their faces
glow like phosphorescent fish
and they cluster together,
shooting straight up like a fountain of light.
Now it is dawn.
We are riding the clouds.
Below us we see the hills
carved out of wood, and the farmers
sanding smooth the little squares of their fields.

4

Washing My Face

Last night's dreams disappear.
They are like the sink draining:
a transparent rose swallowed by its stem.

Lines Written in Dejection, Oklahoma

I have never lived on the reservation.
Let me put it this way: in the web of my hands
I hold an egg of air.
When the girl gets off the train
I will be alone. Only myself and
the moon with its rivers and thorns.

For me there is no getting off.
The river writes my name on its side.
The train with my name on it races
over the dark fields. And the Indian
silhouetted against the ridge
lifts his pony, flings it at the moon.

Manhattan Island Poem

Thin river woman with a concrete star
wedged in her ear. I wrap
a blue scarf of old movies around my eyes.
At night I am a jar of fireflies dying.

Daffodil Poem

I remember the cloud on its blue bicycle
gliding over the leaves under the bare branches.
You and I were walking.
You wore your long green dress
with the hem frayed so the loose threads
seemed like tiny roots.
We were holding hands when my hand
became a yellow scarf
and you stood waving it slowly.
I stepped off the train in Pennsylvania,
just as it began to snow.

8

The Bridge

In the dawn light these white girders
are the bones we want to be free of.

The water calls to me,
saying: Your body is here with us.
Where have you been? We were waiting.
Return to yourself.

Silence

The way the word sinks into the deep snow of the page.

The deer lying dead in the clearing,
its head and antlers transparent.
The black seed in its brain
parachuting toward earth.

The Doll

I carry you in a glass jar.
Your face is porcelain
except for the bullet hole
like a black mole on your cheek.
I want to make you whole again,
but you are growing smaller.
It is almost too late.
When I touch you my fingers
leave dark smudges on your skin.
Each day you are growing
smaller and more intense,
like a drop of acid on my palm;
mothball, snowflake,
dead child.

The Dinner

I invited Mozart to dinner
on condition he didn't
embarrass me.
In the middle of the meal
he began weeping uncontrollably.
"You silly fuck," I screamed,
"what are you doing
in this century
if you can't take it?"

The Wooden Dancer

She wears a necklace of light.
Each bead is a deserted room
you enter: bare light bulb, a white
glove on a table. You walk to the window
and stare out at the snowfields.
A flock of sparrows is eating your footprints.

The Girl with 18 Nightgowns

And each one to the advantage of her breasts
which were present in softness
and under softness
were present
like miniature rabbits in the Andes
that only come out at night.

The Room

With crayons and pieces of paper, I entered the empty room.
I sat on the floor and drew pictures all day.
One day I held a picture against the bare wall:
it was a window. Climbing through,

I stood in a sloping field
at dusk. As I began walking, night settled.
Far ahead in the valley, I saw the lights
of a village, and always at my back I felt
the white room swallowing what was passed.

"Transients Welcome"

To be like the water:
a glass snake asleep in the pipes.
But behind you the dream burns the empty nests,
and before you the day with its ball of twine.
You piss in the sink. Frying pan in hand,
padding down the hall, you turn the corner
and find an old woman asleep on the stove.

The Fast

My bones start singing through my skin.
They sing about the other life
when they had teeth of their own.
It is a lie they heard from their father.
They sing all the old lies
as though they were threats.
They think they can frighten me,
because I grow thin.
But I know my rights.
I know the law, the one that says:
The bones of the son belong to the father.
They are his food.

The Sleeping Angel

All the rooms of the house fill with smoke,
because an angel is sleeping on the chimney.

Outside, black leaves shaped like mouths
lie scattered on the lawn.
Snails, little death-swans,
glide over these dark lakes.

The Ambassadors

With packages of blood
tucked under their arms
and the dubious gifts
of the Emperor hidden in their sleeves,
they stream up the palace steps.
Their silk robes fill
the narrow corridors
and beat against the walls.
They kneel before the prince
and unsheathe the sword of bone:
the wars he will fight
are carved on its blade.

Making Beasts

for Daniel Young

When I was about ten
I glued together an old
white turtle shell,
a woodchuck's skull,
and a red squirrel's tail
to make my first
mythical beast.
What has been created
is never lost. It crawls
up through my thoughts now
on the feet I never gave it.

In an Empty Field at Night

for Peter

A man carries a skull of red yarn
that unravels as he walks.
With his steps he traces
the labyrinth scratched on his palm.
At its center he discovers the tree
whose leaves open underground
and whose white roots toss in the wind.

Poem to the Body

Hollow tree, you are filled with all the hands
that ever touched you.

You dream of the rock falling through space.
You dream about valleys filling with snow,

or about the day your stomach returned
from its long journey. Resting at your feet,
it told a story about the pie your mother baked,
filled with green leaves and your fingers.

Sunrise

I woke up and saw her winding the ropes
tight around the white throat of the house.
She stood on the roof and threw bricks
from the chimney into the river.
I ran outside, screaming:
Come down, old woman!

But she laughed, and hiding her face in one red wing,
she threw me her bracelet, the black candle.

Poem to the Mother

Dead leaves nest in the crown and the word
"yesterday" is like a pile of bones.

But is a volcano ever extinct,
even when its bowl fills with snow
and the giant ice deer come there to die?

Kissing you makes the leaves fall.

How they heaped snow in the cradle
of your hips and it didn't melt.
How at your touch the flowers
exploded in flames.

Again we dismantle the motorcycle.
In your arms you rock the black egg of the gas tank.
A beak like golden pliers tears at the thin metal.
Another you is released into the universe.

Poem for My Dead Mother

Please accept this translation.
It is from a poem written in the language of stones.

I was in the mountains, as though surrounded by mountains,
when you pointed to the dry stream bed.
It was there: a round clay pot
nestled among boulders.

For Brynhilde

I hear you are married again and live
in Syracuse. The scars on your wrists,
like the thin purple lips of the dead,
shrink but do not disappear.

When I first saw you in the school lunchroom,
you could only have been six years my senior,
though you never said. You entered our house

with your mother beside you, swearing in German,
calling us pigs and Jews. There were evenings
you said you loved us, and nights you chased us with knives.

We could have pitied you, but we didn't.
Our mother had been dead two years:
we kids had grown to like the feeling
of a last outpost surrounded.

As I grew older I tried to imagine you in bed,
but you were so tense and brittle
you splintered like dry bones beneath the weight.

And I escaped to college, where the news
of half-hearted suicides and murders meant less.
And then the old man left,

taking my brothers and sister.
You were left alone in the house
like the last of the Nazi soldiers
you said we misunderstood.

Nakedness

I am this tree whose bark is fur
and whose wood is salt.

There is a shirt that devours me.
It is the rain.

Climbing the Falls

Don't look down.
Keep your eyes on handholds
that pock this cliff face
like a thousand empty eye sockets.
If you slipped,
you would fall forever.

Going Out

You hold your hands up to the light.
The small mirrors of your fingernails
are painted over with blood.
You help me knot the black
tie tight around my throat.
Tonight we are going to dine.
We have a hunger that nothing has filled.
It grows large and rigid.
We stand in it like a room.

Beginning

You stand alone in the empty street
and the dark air swept from houses
swirls thickly around your knees.

You remember cutting the white threads,
how a red drop formed like a tear at each end.
But when you cut the black threads, the thicker ones,
there was a sweet heavy smell of flowers and urine.

Now you begin. Because your boots
leave no marks on the hard earth,
you will make each journey many times.

Poem

This life like no other.
The bread rising in the ditches.
The bellies of women swelling
with air.
Walking alone under the dark pines,
a blue leather bridle in my hand.

Waterfall at Night

Throne of black foam.
At its feet a glass heart floats,
filled with worms of light.

Resting on a log, I eat a bowl of snow
with a spoon carved from a bone.
I bite down on something hard and pull it out:
it is a tiny black wheel, my voice.

Poem

One man climbs inside a thorntree
as easily as another man
grows thick fur over his whole body.

But as night descends, each man
moves toward the door. Once outside,
he wraps himself in the cloak of his own shadow.

Arriving by their separate paths, the men
gather along the river bank. They watch
the children dancing on the water,
dressed in robes made of tiny bones.

October

At my feet the stream flows backwards,
a road through the hills,
but to travel it I would have to be naked,
more naked than I have ever been.

Behind me the red and orange leaves whisper.
I am afraid of the woods in daylight,
the colors demanding I feel.

My hands are cold. I am trapped
between the woods and the water.
"I must face this fear," I think,
and struggle to stay in my body, but
the scream comes, the scream
that is like my hands
only larger, like two wings of ice.

3

The Meadow

I sit in the grass as the moon rises.
White deer file out of the woods,
tossing their antlers like branches in a storm.
They leap and their hooves strike
sparks on the stones.
The whole field burns.
I stand in its center. The flames die.
I am a tower of ashes.
Only my eyes remain, two moons,
two pebbles sifting through clouds of warm ash.

Love Poem

A black biplane crashes through the window
of the luncheonette. The pilot climbs down,
removing his leather hood.
He hands me my grandmother's jade ring.
No, it is two robin's eggs and
a telephone number: yours.

For Naoko, Standing Alone
in the Field

Your eyes fixed on the white flowers in the cloud.
The fact that the wind does not stir
your heavy green dress.
At the edge of the field, elm trees
step out in their black armor.
You pause. Around you the swollen
orange seed pods of the jewelweed burst quietly.

Love Poem

We wake up and in the lumps of coal in our hands
black ferns are unrolling.
The room is a hollow tree
with a spiral stair at its center.
We race down through darkness,
our hands on the banister,
white leaves in a whirlpool.
At the bottom we enter the tunnels
which are the roots of light.

Sleepless Night

The night passes, wagon with wheels of black water.
It is heaped with the bodies of glass birds.

Naoko sleeps beside me.
"She is a woman," I tell myself.
"She is not these images you are always seeing.
She wants your arm around her in the darkness.
You want her warmth.
When will you ever learn?"

A Marriage

We were dreaming of the same empty bed;
how clouds trampling on the sheets
with their crystal feet gave the illusion
of its having been slept in.

You sat at the table,
your fingers taking root in the cup of black tea.
I stood by the window
that looks out on the meadow of thorns,
drawing slow circles on the pane.

A Final Aubade

I go out to greet the dawn, dawn
that is a deeper darkness, face
of the woman I love, unknowable mask.

Behind it a river flows over stones
shaped like hands. The dead with their glass legs
walk by the river. The river
seems to pass through them.

Getting Dressed

1

In the morning, I pull on my helmet of skin
backwards. I see what a light bulb sees
through a lampshade.

2

Putting on the white gloves,
the ones with little teeth
that close around my wrists.

3

Pale feet, two corpses that will not stay buried,
I thrust you into my boots:
wearing this barbaric armor
you go out to battle the air, the stones,
the earth that wants to swallow you.

Trying to Sleep

I am too thin.
My bones press against my flesh:
they are trying to break free
and live separate lives like candles.
I try to think of something else.
I sit up and look out the window.
There is only the neighbor's black dog
barking at the snow.

Song of the Salamander

A nest of white fire glows at the top of the hill:
home you have sought all these years.
Dragging your huge muddy tail, you crawl
toward the moon rising through the trees.

ur slow and endless fall
zzard of cigarettes.
paint faces on the stones;
u a ride in their car.
he cards again, pulling
 out of your rib cage.
ry, but what's the use;
lready filled with tears,
bleached logs in the pond in the woods.
for good.

Withdrawing

"Here," she said, but it was a leaf.
"There," she pointed, but it was a stone.
He was lying face down in the lake
and the raw back of the water had become his back.
He was not transparent, far from it.
He was growing darker,
becoming a sky
at night
without stars.

Sleeping Alone in a Small Room

There are dawns when the window is white with moths,
or black with the ink they spin out of their bodies.

I dream of stones covered with snow.
Or I stand on a hill at night,
counting the fires in the valley.
Once I held a blue cup shaped like an hourglass.
Looking into it, past the narrow waist, I saw her
small, child's face staring up from the bottom.

Then there are mornings I wake between darkness and light
and see the cloud that hangs by a rope from the steeple
turn red and begin to dance.

Singing the Pai

I crouch naked at the w
and call its name softly,
until it hovers over me
in its shadow. Then I th
over it, pulling it down
that its body fits perfec
like a fish-shaped cork.
Its wings beat frantically
fold them carefully into
bundle on its back.

For Goc

You begin y
through a b
Your friends
they offer y
You shuffle
damp leave
Wanting to
your bones
floating like
She is gone

4

The Adventures of the Stone

The Stone That Is Fear

The stone sat at a desk lit by a single candle.
The walls of the room, like the inner walls of its body,
were covered with mirrors.
The stone was writing. It looked up occasionally,
staring at the thousand reflected candle flames
that seemed to be points of light perforating a dark sky.
It glanced at its watch that ran on blood.
It returned to its writing.

A Stone's Poem of Pain

In the dark hollow between your lungs, an apple
is growing; a white apple the size of her breasts,
but no one can see it. Only you
feel it pressing out against your ribs,
but the pain is distant, hovers over you
like your mother's hand about to strike.

Remembering Her Kiss

It is night. The stone sits in a field.
It scoops both hands through the grass
and holds them up to the moon.
In the hollow of one hand, a minnow swims.
From the other stares a child's mask made of gold.

The Stone in Winter

The stone lives in a snow house in the woods.
At night, it sits in the cage
the moonlight makes as it falls
through the branches of a leafless tree.

One day a woman came with a flock of tame wolves.
She gave it an arrow of black glass.

The stone has some seeds it is saving;
they are embedded in a block of ice.
Sometimes the stone dreams it is a man
in love with a warm woman.

The Animals

The stone didn't trust the animals.
Why should it? The owls ruled
the night, and the mice were cowards.
The wolves worked for the ice woman.

The snakes were dying.
How long since anyone had seen a deer?
As dusk fell, the stone sat by a deerprint,
months old, still glowing faintly.
The stone nibbled black bread.

The Vampire

The room was dark. Something
touched the stone's neck lightly as lover's fingers.
Waking, the stone felt a gnawing emptiness
as though there was a well filled with blood
which the vampire had emptied;
the stone bent over the well which was itself
and for the first time it knew thirst.

A Late Night Visitor

Even the stone had misunderstood him:
so claimed the tall man, his leathery wings
wrapped like a black cape across his chest.
It was not himself he was feeding,
and he unfolded one wing to reveal
a tiny female doll where his heart should have been.
He explained: her mouth is like one of those trick bowls
magicians use; no matter how much
milk you pour into it, it appears empty.
Even he could not solve the puzzle of her thirst.

The stone eyed him carefully. Something was amiss.
Then it saw its visitor reflected in the mirror
and thin wires rising from his body.
The stone saw itself straddling a small cloud
near the ceiling, pulling the wires.

The Clearing

The vampire stalked among the trees, and the stone
shadowed him. He passed a circle
of witches dancing around a fire.
He passed any number of potential victims
and continued threading his way through the forest.
It was almost dawn when they reached the clearing.
As the vampire approached the pond at its center,
the stone suddenly remembered: this was its own birthplace!
In the gray light, the vampire stood on a small cliff
above the pond. He dove and in middive became
a black stone tumbling toward a mirror.

Concerning the Stone

The stone went out, dressed as a man.
At the party, the stone danced.
Late at night in the park, the stone
pressed its mouth to the damp earth.
The stone did not cry, but periodically
the gray bowls of its hands would fill with tears.
It carried a stick to beat away
the clouds. It carried a mirror
to remind itself. Having seen the woman once,
the stone could not close the wound
or make it speak.

Late at Night

As the stone wrote, ants swarmed over its feet.
It was trying to write a story that began:
"The wound is the only cup
from which to drink clear water."
It heard a far-off singing. Turning, it saw the woman
dancing barefoot on a circle of ground glass.
It wanted its hands and its feet to drop off.
It wanted to curl up in a ball.
But then it heard her voice and she was saying:
"The wound is not a cradle to lie down in."

A Courting Poem

The wound sought out the stone, because
it was tired of living alone and formless
like a cloud in a cave.

But the stone feared the wound,
sensing that it was not like other things
that were there and then gone.
The stone needed the wound, but still

the silence would never be the same again,
because of the hum of blood in its veins.
The long walks after the first snowfall
would be different: now there would be footprints.

At the Wedding in the Woods

Someone brought as a gift the mask made of ice
that the moon had worn; face of the stone's mother,
it fed the mask to the bonfire in the clearing.
Under the trees, tables were heaped with food.
People laughed and chattered. A man
from the local paper saw it this way:
"The stone and the wound danced in a circle of moonlight."

After the Marriage

for Stanley Kunitz

The stone struggled to love the wound,
but its whole body shuddered with loathing.
The stone tore at the wound,
which grew to a red door
through which the stone entered its own body.
It saw a clearing where a white tree grew.
Instead of leaves, there were children
trapped inside glass teardrops.

A Parable

The stone strikes the body, because
that is what stones will do.
The wound opens after the stone's kiss,
too late to swallow the stone.
The wound and the stone become lovers.
The wound owes its life to the stone
and sings the stone's praises.
The stone is moved. At the stone's center,
a red hollow aches to touch the wound.
The gray walls of its body tear open
and the wound enters to dwell there.

A stranger picks up the stone
with the wound inside and carries it
with him until he dies.

About the Author

GREGORY ORR was born in 1947 and raised in
the rural Hudson River Valley in upstate New
York. He was educated at Hamilton College,
Antioch College (B.A., 1969), and Columbia
University School of the Arts (M.F.A.). In
1970, he won the Academy of American
Poets Prize at Columbia and the YM-YWHA
Poetry Center's Discovery Award. He is cur-
rently living in Ann Arbor, Michigan, and is a
Junior Fellow in the University of Michigan
Society of Fellows.

73 74 75 76 77 10 9 8 7 6 5 4 3 2 1